DOLLS AND DOLLS' HOUSES
A COLLECTOR'S INTRODUCTION

by Roger Baker
with a foreword by Patrick Murray M.B.E., F.S.A.Scot.,
Curator of the Museum of Childhood, Edinburgh

ORBIS BOOKS
LONDON

Contents

The following photographs were taken by Iain Macmillan at the Museum of Childhood, Edinburgh (1, 2, 3, 22, 23, 24, 27, 30, 31, 32, 33, 34, 35, 36, 37, 38, 39, 40, 41, 42, 43, 44, 45, 46, 47, 48, 49, 51, 52, 54, 55, 56, 57, 58, 59, 60, 69, 70, 71, 72, 73, 74, 75, 76, 77, 78, 79, 80, 81, 82, 83, 84, 85, 86, 87, 88, 89, 90, 91, 92, 93, 94, 95, 96, 97, 99, 100, 101, 103, 104); at Bethnal Green Museum, London (7, 16, 18, 20, 25, 26, 28, 29, 50, 62, 64, 65, 67, 98); at the London Museum (4, 9, 21); at Sotheby & Co., London (17, 19, 61, 63, 66, 68, 86); and at the Victoria and Albert Museum, London (8, 10).
5: courtesy of the National Gallery, London. 6: courtesy of the Rijksmuseum, Amsterdam. 11, 12, 15: courtesy of the Musée des Arts Décoratifs, Paris. 13, 14, 53: courtesy of the Rotunda Dolls' House Museum, Oxford/Phoebus Picture Library, London.

© Istituto Geografico de Agostini, Novara 1973
English edition © Orbis Publishing Limited, London 1973
Phototypeset in England by Petty and Sons Ltd, Leeds
Printed in Italy by IGDA, Novara
ISBN 0 85613 162 8

Foreword

There is today an entirely novel general public interest – intelligent interest – in dolls and dolls' houses – a most interesting point which Roger Baker highlights here. He also justly draws attention to the sudden growth of doll-collecting as a recognized and acceptable hobby. Isolated doll-collectors there have always been. Long before World War I and perhaps as far away as the beginning of the 19th century such collectors probably existed. But it is certain that collections of dolls begin to be noticed about the 1880s; though the motives prompting some of the collectors would make you shudder. Sadly, it must be confessed, the 'precious' is still with us where dolls are concerned.

But – and they are vastly in the majority – sensible adults are finding in doll-collecting a genuinely adult interest and are developing an awareness that there is very much more behind even the simplest doll than some of our alleged experts on child behaviour would have us believe.

The view that a doll is perhaps one of the most complex of human concepts was tentatively suggested by Edward Lovett over 70 years ago. We now suspect that, quite unwittingly, he stumbled on some of the important implications of dolls. He may have developed some of his ideas in writings now lost; all I happen to have is his catalogue of an exhibition of dolls in Cardiff in 1914, and a small booklet plainly deriving from it.

Since quite a few of his dolls are among those beautifully illustrated in this book it is worth looking at the challenging implications of Lovett's attitude to dolls. His method of offering children manufactured dolls in exchange for the priceless collection of slumland dolls now owned by the Museum of Childhood clearly tests the old theory that 'simple' toys are best-loved. (As though we knew what 'simplicity' in toys means!) Lovett's clients, fleetingly glimpsed in slum streets, at Punch and Judy shows or in fair-grounds, obviously had their own ideas about such hoary nonsense. Simple toys are not necessarily best for every child. Certainly not for the small geniuses whose work we now own.

Lovett's extension of doll-collecting into what was then considered a very way-out field uncovers some more thought-provoking information. Vast as his collection was for those days it has some extraordinary gaps. Or has it? It contains very few baby dolls, and most of those it does contain are Oriental. We are now beginning to realize that the 'maternity' theory behind children's love of dolls does not go far enough. We know that baby dolls are a comparatively modern invention and were almost unknown before London's Great Exhibition of 1851. The doll must represent other urges than that of motherhood; or were little girls before 1851 not interested in their future role?

Other curious gaps in this collection go far towards an explanation of what the doll is all about. Ignoring the fact that not all races have dolls, which jolts the theory that dolls appeal to a maternal instinct, these gaps can be fairly simply explained. His collection has no little girl dolls; the only male dolls were obviously not originally intended to be male. There are no soft dolls other than the slumland toys which have clearly been conditioned by the materials available. The vast majority of the dolls are adult, feminine figures. In other words they reflect the doll world as a whole.

Little girl dolls have existed, although there were very few of them before the early 1900s. They are a very small percentage of the total number of dolls produced. Male dolls also account for only a fraction of all dolls produced; even less when the manufacturer's original intentions are examined. However, *puppenstube* male dolls do survive from the 1890s. These male dolls were produced in Germany to play male parts in dolls' house games. They took their name from the single miniature open room, the *puppenstube*. They were usually handsome in 'blond beast' style. (Ethel Merman in *Call Me Madam* refers to one of the male players as a 'doll'.)

The last kind of doll missing from Lovett's collection is the soft doll. In one-offs soft dolls have always been made throughout the ages, but mass-production of them was not considered sufficiently profitable until techniques of fabric printing were improved in the 1880s. Yet the soft doll, impressionable, sensitive to manipulation and caresses, should be the one thing that any child obeying maternal instincts would demand. If the maternal instinct has anything to do with the doll, that is.

Come to that, is any doll really comfortable to handle?

Not on your life! And never has been.

Dolls, especially those that are collector's items, are so often overweighted; fragile; almost impossible to manipulate (except by small girls, apparently); a mass of awkward limbs and stiff joints; wildly out of proportion; hard and unsympathetic; and in general so utterly unappealing to all that is tender in a woman that it's a wonder to me no manufacturer has yet tried to get away with a doll made of masonry.

But what of the positive side of all these contradictions? Other than that you can't be positive about children – and as I live at close quarters with some 45,000 children throughout the year at the Museum of Childhood I can be positive about that – a clear picture emerges. Dolls down the ages have always been positive; have always reflected adult life to the child; have always needed to be accurate.

You will be very lucky to find a really good doll of the earliest kinds with its original costume complete. Why? Because even if it survives the shiftless feminine passion for change of its first owner, it has then got to survive her daughter. Generally that moppet takes one look at her mother's clothes, another look at the doll's and asks who thinks she's kidding whom. She, the daughter, is not interested in what they wore in the ark, and so . . .

The same applies to dolls' wigs. There is a fortune waiting for any doll repairer who comes upon a forgotten hoard of dolls' wigs dating from before 1918. For in that year and in succeeding years the despotism of the bob, the bingle and the shingle caused every nursery floor to be strewn with the massacred locks of earlier hair-dos.

Lastly we come to the Strange Case of the Dressing Doll. Lovett secured many a lavishly dressed doll: some were made by French couturiers; others achieved in the nursery. But they always represent adults – as very many still do today.

It would seem that in this one, very early collection of dolls some, if not all, of the welter of human needs, vanities, hopes and fears that lie behind the popularity of the doll are to be found. The doll represents not just one human need but a lot. A devil of a lot. Even the baser traits of human nature are represented in this collection which includes a genuine 'waxen poppet' – the black magic doll. And literature affords us a revealing view of just how beastly children can be with their dolls. Some of our most respected literary figures . . . ! Deplorable!

Between the earliest collectors and the collectors of today for whom Roger Baker is writing, then, the doll can be seen to be both an enchanting plaything and an object with a social significance which we are only just beginning to fathom.

One thing remains certain, however – give a child a doll and she will get to work on its appearance.

Patrick Murray M.B.E., F.S.A.Scot.

French fashion doll of the 19th century

Collecting dolls

A serious interest in dolls that were made before the first quarter of this century has developed significantly since World War II. It seems that Americans were the first to seek out, categorize and collect dolls. One British collector, Kay Desmonde, has written that doll-collecting is 'the second most popular hobby in the United States'. Certainly some of the most detailed and authoritative books on the subject have been produced by American collectors.

Today some dolls rank with other antiques in both price-range and scarcity value. Many museums which had considerable collections of dolls tended in the past to give preference to displays of, for example, Roman coins or Saracen swords, but now that interest in dolls has been revived they are dusting and repairing their collections of dolls and putting them on display. We have to thank a small but growing band of enthusiasts for this; in both America and Great Britain there are flourishing dolls' clubs.

Dolls have not always been used as toys for children. They have been totem figures invested with magical properties; symbols of humans in different rites; and display models for fashion merchandise. Dolls that are of interest to the collector, however, are usually those made during the 19th century, although some later dolls do have a certain interest. One reason for this is that dolls made before 1800 are comparatively rare; their age alone guarantees a recognition as an artefact of antique status which is unrelated to any specialist interest in dolls as such.

Although dolls of the 19th century were often mass-produced – the output of the famous Jumeau factory in France rose from 85,000 in 1881 to 220,000 in 1884 – they did have the individual stamp of the artist about them, as did factory-produced china, glass and cutlery. But whereas today china, glass and cutlery of a remarkably high standard are still produced for those dismayed by the mass-product, the same has not happened with dolls.

As an example of the esteem in which antique dolls are held by collectors today, it is worth glancing at the catalogue of a sale of dolls held at Sotheby's, the famous London firm of auctioneers, in December 1972. Prices began at £15 and reached £55 for an English Victorian doll, £130 for a German mid-19th century doll and £550 for a pair of 19th century pedlar dolls. The star of the sale was a George III English painted wooden doll which was bought for £1,000 – a record auction price.

In case anyone should imagine that one doll is much like another, consider the details required by the advanced collector in order to date, classify, and probably to price a doll. A form prepared by an American collector, Mrs Clay Gerken of Nebraska, and called 'Taxonomy of Papier Mâchés' asks for more than 400 details about any single item. The type of material, modelling, head, colouring of the complexion, style in which the face is drawn, materials used for hair, teeth, eyes, hands and arms are required (and there are several possibilities for each) as well as such details as height, clothes and known history.

The ordinary collector is unlikely to be so precise in his or her demands but it is salutary to realize the extent to which objects that are generally regarded as toys, and therefore thought to have a limited life-span, have been elevated by collectors. It is also interesting to see that doll-collecting is a far from exhausted field. Shops specializing in dolls have opened, in London at least, only recently, and there must be many attics, lumber rooms and trunks housing long-forgotten family toys. The chance that a house lived in by the same family for a number of years will contain a fine and valuable doll is much greater than the chance that it will contain an important painting.

Early dolls

The Concise Oxford Dictionary defines 'doll' as 'toy baby', which is only one aspect of its definition. However, it adds, as an alternative, 'puppet' which is further defined as 'figure, usually small, representing human being.' The word puppet derives from the Middle English *popette*

Doll-makers of the 17th century at work

which is related to the French word *poupette* which means, of course, doll. The classical Greek word for a wax doll was *plangon* which seems to have survived only in the term plangonologist – a doll-collector.

The word doll has, it seems, only been used since the 17th century to mean a small figure, and it derives from a diminutive of the proper name Dorothy. It has been suggested that pedlars selling puppets probably began to refer to their wares in this way. In Elizabethan drama characters named Doll are usually pretty, cheeky women of low social status, like Shakespeare's Doll Tearsheet or Ben Jonson's Doll Common.

As far as the origin of the word itself goes the history of dolls should be considered from the 17th century onwards. But dolls have existed for centuries although they have not always played the role they do today. The excavation of ancient sites has produced some small representations of the human figure; these have been discovered all over the European continent and date from different times, being of Greek, Roman, Egyptian, Gallic and British origins. Variously made from clay, wood, bone or terracotta, they are usually called dolls although their function was usually more serious than the simple amusement of children.

These small representations of the human figure were almost certainly held to possess magical qualities. In Ancient Egyptian, and in some African, rituals of death and burial doll-figures were used. Sometimes, as in the ego-oriented religious practices of Egypt, they may represent the dead person, or they may symbolize his family and friends, suggesting an assurance that he is not being abandoned by them in death. They could be placed in the grave as guardians, or set in the home of the deceased person, representing his spirit and thus helping its difficult transfer from this world to the next. There was a nautical tradition which lasted until the present century whereby if a sailor was lost at sea in battle or storm a doll representing him was either put under the doorway of his house or given a ceremonial burial in a false grave.

The use of dolls in witchcraft to cause pain or even death to a specified person is well known. These dolls could be formed of any material but were usually of wax. They had to incorporate some part of the proposed victim, such as a strand of hair or a nail-paring. Witchcraft dolls were also employed in spells to bring two people together in love or a sexual bond. They may still be found today, especially in countries which have a long history of magic and fetishism.

Ancient dolls were often fertility figures. Barren wives used them to encourage pregnancy, and whole communities used them to give thanks for a successful harvest or to propitiate the gods and ensure a fruitful crop. Corn dollies are still made in many rural areas at harvest time.

Dolls created for adult purposes are more likely to survive than dolls made for children to play with. Nevertheless, enough fragile dolls have survived to indicate that children have always had dolls, although it is debatable whether the children of Ancient Greece and Rome played with them in the same way as modern children. So much depends on the way in which children were treated in a particular culture – a point to which we shall return. Dolls of Ancient Egyptian origin have been discovered made from ivory, wax and even fabric. At the excavation at Antenore a doll was unearthed with a wooden head, a rag body and movable arms; and the British Museum has a rag doll of Roman origin. Greek and Roman dolls have been found with movable limbs so they could be dressed; they were sometimes painted with cosmetics just like the more sophisticated Roman ladies. Even in these civilizations dolls were sometimes rudimentary, made for children to toss around in the street or courtyard, and sometimes beautifully made to please discerning adults. Dolls enjoyed a popularity in Roman times that was not revived until the 19th century. In between, the idea of an industry created solely to supply children with playthings remained an alien concept. For the history of modern dolls you have to look to medieval Europe.

6

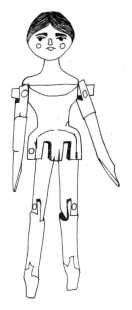

Traditional Dutch doll

Wooden, papier mâché, wax and china dolls

The German town of Nuremberg has been associated with dolls since the Middle Ages. Dolls dressed in clothes of the 14th century have been discovered there but they were made of clay; the most important characteristic of Nuremberg's dolls and toys has been their use of wood. Since the surrounding districts of Nuremberg are heavily wooded a tradition of highly skilled ecclesiastical woodcarving sprang up and was soon extended into the production of all sorts of toys, small carved objects and dolls. Nuremberg retained its supremacy as the toy-making centre for Europe for centuries, rivalled only by Sonneberg, another German town with a history of toy-making.

Documentation relating to the making and distribution of dolls during the 14th, 15th and 16th centuries is scarce. Portraits of royalty and the aristocracy sometimes show a doll, which is usually a very formal figure. The great fairs which were held all over Europe provided an opportunity for dolls to be seen and sold as did travelling pedlars.

Until the 18th century wood was certainly the main material used for dolls. There are records of the use of wax, glazed stoneware and even alabaster and gold for dolls in the 17th century but these dolls were probably intended for décor not play. Early wooden dolls, many of which can still be seen in museums and private collections, are well made, carefully jointed creatures. The earliest surviving wooden dolls are carved from one piece of wood, clothes as well, but later the concept of dressing was applied to them, and their clothes were always exact copies of the adult female dress of the period, giving them a stiff, rather formal appearance.

By the 18th century the distribution of dolls had developed into a full-scale industry. Already doll-makers in Nuremberg and Sonneberg had been granted exemptions from taxes and duties equal to those accorded the merchants at their public markets. A system of agents had been set up to distribute German dolls throughout Europe and the first recorded private request for dolls from America was in 1695. The familiar expression 'Dutch doll' does not always refer to a doll made in Holland but is a corruption of *Deutsch*, showing how popular German dolls were all over Europe. Queen Victoria possessed a collection of such wooden dolls which she dressed to imitate famous figures. By about 1820 the ball-and-socket joints which had characterized wooden dolls and which held the limbs firmly to the body were replaced by more flimsy joints. As often happens, when short cuts were taken in production quality deteriorated.

New techniques in doll-making emerged from the Industrial Revolution, heralding the age of mass-production. A new and larger market for toys and dolls was being created. The major breakthrough in technique at this time was the use of papier mâché for dolls. This combination of mashed paper, glue and a thickening agent (plaster or leather scrapings) though long known to the Chinese was unknown in Europe until the beginning of the 18th century. By the 19th century the Germans applied the technique to toy-making. Papier mâché could be made quickly and cheaply and was ideal for dolls' heads; it had the advantages of being easy to mould and almost impossible to break.

Dolls' bodies were made from a variety of materials – kid, fabric, wood or even earthenware. Today these bodies are usually in poor condition while the papier mâché heads retain their original charm. Much sought-after are those that reproduce the elaborate hair-styles of the early 19th century with clusters of ringlets bunched high on either side of the head. For this reason they are sometimes known as 'milliner's dolls'.

Another technique, originally developed in Germany but soon imitated, was to dip papier mâché heads into wax. If the head was moulded and then painted the layers of wax would lend it a particularly delicate texture and colour. Unfortunately the thin wax tended to crack and chip and many a surviving doll has her ladylike appearance somewhat diminished by a missing nose or fractured

7

Fortune-telling doll of the 18th century; her skirt is made of folded papers on which fortunes are written

forehead. Technically these dolls are known as 'wax over composition'.

England has never been an important doll-making country and has produced only one character doll, the pedlar doll. It did, however, lead the world in the manufacture of wax dolls, producing dolls with both head and limbs moulded from pure wax. Liquid wax was poured into moulds to form these expensive and individually finished works of art. One famous doll-maker who sold the moulds and glass eyes for such dolls was a Mrs Salmon who died in 1760 at the age of 90.

The finished heads and limbs were attached to a fabric body which gave them mobility. Hair was set into the head and eyebrows, while the finishing touches were the delicate painting of the features and polishing of the cheeks. The wax was not solid, consisting of a layer over a form, but gave the doll a singularly attractive glow.

Italy, like England, produced doll-makers rather than one particular tradition of doll-making. The Pierotti family who specialized in wax dolls produced dolls of a very high quality much prized by collectors today. The family settled in England in the late 18th century, and the last member retired from the family business in 1935. Another celebrated doll-maker was Madame Augusta Montanari who produced spectacularly lovely creatures in a high price-range. French experts in the mid-19th century judged that wax busts from England scored top marks for delicacy, but insisted that those made in France were modelled more realistically.

In the 1830s doll-makers began to use china for dolls' heads. The earliest ones were produced by the great porcelain factories of Meissen and Royal Copenhagen; as might be expected these are considered the most exquisite. It is likely that production of separate heads for dolls began as another outlet for the elegant range of ornaments and *objets d'art* that were being produced. It was soon realized that china looked delicate but was surprisingly tough. Later Parian and bisque (unglazed china) were used for decorative objects and, as before, the makers followed this by using the same materials for

dolls' heads. Parian became particularly popular as its modelling was sharp; it was used for portrait dolls. The royal family of England, the Empress of France and Napoleon III were thus portrayed, always with an attractive attention to detail of facial features and costume. Portrait dolls are still made today.

A taxonomy of dolls produced by the jury of the 1849 Paris Exposition indicates what was demanded at the time. A doll, they said, consists of ten pieces: a bust of wax or composition; a body, sometimes of cardboard, sometimes stuffed with sawdust and covered with a kid skin; teeth of straw or enamel; eyes, painted or of glass or enamel; hands of wood, composition or yellow skin; hair, curled or coiffed; stockings and underwear; complete toilette; a hat; shoes. The production of each separate item was entrusted to a specialist.

The great expositions and exhibitions with which the 19th century celebrated its industrial growth and commercial prowess were splendid opportunities for doll-makers. From about 1850 the industry displayed astounding growth, with Germany and France the chief competitors, but the English dolls were praised at the first International Exhibition in 1851: 'the doll with the well-made body was indeed French, but the doll with the elegant head and the pretty face was certainly English.'

Until this time no particular distinction had been made between dolls representing babies and dolls representing adults. At the Great Exhibition held in London in 1851 Madame Montanari displayed dolls that were clearly of different ages. Her highly realistic babies caused concern at first but were soon accepted and imitated.

Another curiosity that first appeared on the market in 1850 was the doll known as a 'frozen Charlotte'. These were all-china dolls without joints and are also known as pillar dolls and pudding dolls. Usually they were tiny although some were made up to 18 inches tall. The name derives from an American ballad of the early 19th century about 'fair Charlotte' who went out into the snow with no coat in order to show off her dress; unfortunately she was frozen rigid almost immediately.

Dressed Kewpie doll

Innovation and experiment

The last half of the 19th century is a story of invention and experiment in response to the increasing need to improve and vary the range and abilities of dolls. The French tended to specialize in mechanical and novelty dolls, although the first walking doll was actually an American invention called the Autoperipatetikos. Musical boxes incorporated into dolls enabled them to sing, and clockwork mechanisms were also introduced.

Eventually the French took the lead in producing the most elegant and best dressed dolls. Leading doll-makers established themselves in Paris, including the firm of Casimir Bru which started in 1866 and, perhaps most famous of all, the Jumeau factory which became the largest doll-making establishment in the world. Jumeau continually won prizes at exhibitions for his dolls and was constantly developing his product. In 1873 Emile Jumeau was using porcelain heads made at Montreuil-sous-Bois which were considered better than those which could be imported from Germany. The French firms specialized in what are known as *'bébés'* – child-dolls rather than actual babies. Everything about them from their luxuriant wigs to their neat, buckled shoes was impeccable, and they were large enough to allow for their being dressed in the height of fashion.

These lovely dolls are sometimes known as *Parisiennes* and sometimes as 'fashion' dolls. This last term is now generally used to indicate a particularly well-dressed doll of French origin, and it has been suggested that they were used by couturiers to display and spread the latest designs. Certainly the self-conscious French knew that their dolls made good ambassadors; 'it is partly through dolls that most people of the two hemispheres know France and are familiar with her customs, her ideas and her costumes. If one opened a case destined for Valparaiso, Mexico or Smyrna one would find an assortment there that would include some girls of the lower classes, some peasants, some sutlers, some rabble-rousers, some grand ladies in wedding outfits, in town clothes or in ball-gowns, some

queens, some marquises of the last century.' Fashion dolls were first used during the reign of Louis XIV and did indeed help to spread French fashions across Europe. The first figures were probably almost the size of a fully grown adult and their dress was correct in every detail; it is doubtful whether the smaller dolls of the mid-19th century were used for anything more than to give a general guide to the home dress-maker.

These superb dolls were not, of course, for everyone; only the wealthy could afford one of Madame Montanari's fully dressed dolls or a real Jumeau *bébé*. Most children had to be content with the simple wooden figures such as those the young Queen Victoria dressed. One very popular figure was the pedlar doll which was a British invention and dates from the late 18th century. Originally made at home, these dolls were clearly inspired by the wandering pedlars who sold an enormous variety of goods throughout the country. The trays or baskets carried by the dolls were stocked with innumerable miniature objects such as song-sheets, knitted garments, ribbons, pins, glass and china. Today they are greatly prized and fetch high prices when they come onto the market.

In her enchanting memoir *A Victorian Nursery* Winifred Gwyn-Jeffreys describes her life as a child in the 1870s. 'We had very few toys,' she writes, 'a doll apiece for the girls, and bricks for the boys.' Theirs was a large, professional-class household. She adds: 'we had a large school on the nursery floor, which was attended by paper dolls cut from fashion papers.'

Children and dolls

The world of dolls and doll-collecting might seem to offer a pleasant hobby for nice ladies but the amateur collector needs to have the sort of hard-headed preoccupation with dates and makers' marks evidenced in the taxonomy already referred to. Even so the hobby tends to have overtones of sentimentality regarding children or an indulgence in luxury related to the dolls themselves. Both these attitudes obscure certain social realities which are

Early 20th century novelty dolls

relevant to dolls as a phenomenon rather than to the collection of dolls as a pastime.

It was not until the end of the 18th century that ideas about children underwent a radical change; until then children had been regarded as miniature adults with few special needs of their own. We know from the paintings of Breughel and other artists that children had toys and played games but these were very simple and of an extrovert nature. By the 19th century more conscious effort was being put into the creation of a special world for children. The same attitude brought an end to the exploitation of children in industry and fostered the growth of imaginative, as opposed to pious or instructive, literature for children; it also brought full development to the toy industry. Less attractive was the accompanying tendency to treat children themselves like dolls – as spoiled, petted, pretty objects, speaking only when spoken to and forever on their best behaviour.

During the 19th century dolls were increasingly made to resemble human beings, a development aided by improvements in technology. Dolls that were meant to imitate babies were made to look wrinkled and slightly cross like real babies – a development that originated in Germany at the beginning of this century. Dolls were made to walk on their own, to utter squeaks when hugged (to speak when spoken to) and even to swim. This development has been brought to its logical conclusion in the 20th century with the creation of a doll that will urinate. The American writer Terry Southern wove a short fantasy round a doll that menstruated – an idea that may seem distasteful but gives rise to some thoughts on the function of the doll in today's society.

Although beautiful, luxuriously dressed dolls were produced in ever-greater quantities, children have always been able to create their own dolls from whatever materials were available. Dolls often seem to have been designed to please adults rather than the children they were aimed at. Scotland's unrivalled Museum of Childhood in Edinburgh houses a remarkable collection of slumland toys which includes many dolls. They were collected from the children who made them and have been dubbed by the curator of the museum, Patrick Murray, 'emergent' dolls since they emerged according to the child's needs and the materials available. All these dolls reveal an imaginative and touching use of everyday objects; one, for example, is formed from a shoe.

In his interesting book *Toys* Patrick Murray describes how Edward Lovett collected the emergent dolls by offering children 'flashy' shop-bought dolls in exchange. He writes: 'my bet is that he was successful in half his bids. The extroverted child would gladly take the new doll. She recognized it, even if unaware, as a step in her development; a stronger step towards her horizon of privileged adulthood. On the other hand, the introverted child would refuse the exchange. She had come to terms with her toys, and she wanted nothing changed in them.' It is doubtful whether a collection of emergent dolls will ever be sold at Sotheby's, but their existence is a useful reminder that dolls do not have to be beautiful or expensive to have meaning for a child.

Few dolls were produced in America until after the Civil War although dolls were imported from Europe as early as the 17th century. During the latter part of the 19th century Philadelphia, Cincinnati and New York were producing indigenous dolls. Eventually New York became the leading centre as immigrants from Europe settled there bringing doll-making skills with them.

In recent years modern American dolls have become known all over the world as indeed have so many products from the United States. American dolls have usually been either very glamorous, semi-adult dolls with changes of fashionable clothing, or have been reproductions of charming babies. They reflect, in fact, certain values in 20th century society and seem aimed primarily at suggesting to young girls both the virtues of motherhood and the devices of adult female artifice. At first glance there may seem no particular difference between any of today's plastic dressing dolls and a fashionably dressed mid-19th century doll. Both represent standards of contemporary beauty. But the earlier example

Mid-18th century dolls' house from Holland

concentrates its attractiveness (apart from a delicately sculptured face) on the dress. The modern doll repeats the adult female shape and make-up. A few years ago one doll manufacturer hit on the idea of making dolls which showed the genitals of both sexes. This was not popular and the model seems to have been taken off the market.

Perhaps the most interesting example of the modern baby doll is the Bye-Lo baby which was designed by an art teacher in California called Grace Storey Putnam. She spent several weeks looking for the perfect baby on which to model her doll. It was a tremendous success and newspapers began to call it 'the million-dollar baby'. This was in the 1920s; examples are rare today.

Naturally, the increased range of materials produced in the 20th century has enabled dolls to be made in all kinds of substances. Rubber was used experimentally for dolls' heads as early as 1840, but it was not until the 1920s that rubber dolls were produced and accepted in a big way. At this time emphasis was being placed on the importance to growing children of correct 'doll-play', which really amounted to children being encouraged to treat their dolls as real babies, to practise feeding, nappy-changing, bathing and so on. Rubber was suitable for these things.

Celluloid (which dents easily and is inflammable) has also been used and in recent years plastic and vinyl, which are cheap to produce, have been popular. Most of the plump, pink, fancily dressed dolls in department stores are made of vinyl. The Kewpie doll with its cheeky face and grin was an American invention of 1913 made of celluloid.

The themes of baby and of glamorous young adult are those most frequently repeated in contemporary dolls. There have been some experiments, one of the most successful being the Action Man doll which was created for boys – an aggressive, modern doll. The most recent arrival on the market is Daisy designed by the leading fashion designer Mary Quant. Daisy, who is nine inches high, is sleek, leggy and blonde and could properly be called a modern fashion doll. She possesses 36 different outfits to take her through a fairly hectic social scene.

Dolls' houses

Most people associate dolls with dolls' houses; both are, of course, small imitations of a larger reality and tend to be considered essentially playthings for children, particularly girls. This can, however, be a rather misleading line of thought, for beyond these simple facts there is little formal correlation between the two items. A *doll* is a highly personal possession and its character and function are dictated by the needs of its owner, whereas a *dolls' house* has a more extrovert appeal. Clearly most dolls are too large to be played with in conjunction with dolls' houses. The difference in scale will eventually disturb even the most imaginative children, so special tiny dolls were made to go with the exquisitely detailed rooms of dolls' houses. Whole families of dolls remain associated with their houses, often complete with a large staff.

In human terms, then, dolls may be said to appeal primarily to the emotions while dolls' houses appeal more to the intellect and involve adult disciplines of discrimination and order.

For the collector the dolls' house implies a very wide field of interest which embraces social history and the arts. Dolls' houses are a comparatively recent phenomenon and do not share the history of dolls although both have entered the sphere of the collector.

The first dolls' houses

The earliest examples of what we would recognize today as a dolls' house were hardly toys for children. The Nuremberg kitchen is usually held to be the forerunner of the dolls' house. Nuremberg kitchens were models of 17th century German kitchens complete with a miniature *batterie de cuisine*; some even had ovens which worked. These individual kitchens are associated with Nuremberg since many were made there but they were also produced in Holland and elsewhere in Europe. The Museum of Childhood in Edinburgh contains a so-called Nuremberg

Detail of a typical Nuremberg kitchen

kitchen which was made in America and imported to Britain at the end of the 19th century. The precise function of these superbly detailed models is uncertain. Patrick Murray of this Museum of Childhood states quite simply that they were Dutch 17th century domestic science toys. Certainly the accuracy of the models and the wide range of equipment they contained indicates a serious motive behind their manufacture, and it is generally accepted that they were used to instruct girls in the art of kitchen management.

Other individual rooms were created at the same time; models of elegant 17th century drawing rooms and bedrooms still exist. They, too, were reproduced with loving attention to detail and contain small figures to complete the representation just as Nuremberg kitchens housed busy cooks. These rooms were not intended to provide instruction for children but were made to display the work of craftsmen in miniature. The 17th century saw a rising interest in miniature objects particularly furniture but also china and glass, silver and other domestic goods. The high standard of craftsmanship needed to execute this exacting and detailed work, coupled with an unstinting use of materials, means that such collections of miniature objects are not only valuable today but a delight to acquire.

Commenting on these room-settings, Patrick Murray writes: 'it took the pragmatical mid-18th century English to penetrate the implication and make the clusters look like houses.' Collections of individual rooms grouped together could only have been made by the wealthy and leisured; these were the people with country houses and large estates who could readily employ their own carpenters and cabinet-makers. So the English baby-house, as these new pieces of furniture were called, came into being. One notable baby-house, at Nostell Priory in Yorkshire, was built by the estate carpenter in 1740. It was built to look like the main house, whose architect was James Paine, with similar Ionic columns and pediment. Vivien Greene, England's most famous collector of dolls' houses and a leading expert on them,

has suggested that the Nostell carpenter was Thomas Chippendale whose furniture is one of the glories of England's 18th century craftsmanship. Chippendale certainly supplied the miniature furniture for another baby-house which was made in his London workshops for the Vanderstegen family of Cane End near Reading. This beautiful baby-house has a superb staircase; unfortunately the furniture is no longer with the house (which is in Mrs Greene's Rotunda Museum at Oxford).

The earliest baby-houses were essentially display cabinets designed to accommodate collections of miniatures; they were placed in the drawing room, not the nursery, and ranked in visual appeal with all the other *objets d'art* displayed in wealthy homes. Usually they are large and heavy, and made from oak or mahogany. They open like cupboards; the entire façade may act as a door, there may be only one section to open, or there may be three separate sections. In every case the cabinet is fitted with a reliable lock. To display their contents to their best advantage baby-houses had to be placed on a table or possess a stand. The early examples usually incorporate a table in the piece either as a base with cupboards or quite simply as legs.

Dutch baby-houses followed the same pattern of development and bear a strong similarity to English baby-houses of the same period. As yet very little attention was paid to resemblance to real houses in either country. Domestic and architectural essentials such as a staircase or a proper roof with chimneys, were not included. The cupboard doors were sometimes made to look like the façade of a house with windows, pediment and front door, but were usually finished at the top by a simple balustrade hiding a flat, sometimes removable, roof. The somewhat austere line of neoclassical 18th century architecture prevalent in England and Holland influenced the design of early baby-houses.

The crèche, which also originated in the 18th century, has been seen as another forerunner of the dolls' house. The French seem to have taken delight in models of scenes representing birth, not only the Nativity but also

Type of dolls' house played with by Queen Victoria

the more immediately familiar domestic episodes. Like the Nuremberg kitchens these crèches may have been used to give children an introduction to an important aspect of adult life. Many of these little scenes are very attractive, notably those made in glass at Nevers.

From furniture to toy

Although 18th century baby-houses were designed to appeal to adults, children were by no means excluded from enjoying them or from taking an active part in their furnishing and decoration. One of the oldest surviving baby-houses in England, which is in the Strangers' Hall Museum in Norwich, is known to have been given by Queen Anne to her god-daughter Ann Sharp who was the daughter of the Archbishop of York; and the Uppark baby-house was originally owned by a child, Sarah Lethieullier, who took it with her to Uppark when she married.

During the closing years of the 18th century the baby-house began slowly to evolve from furniture to toy. The first sign of this comes when exteriors were made more realistic; brightly coloured brickwork was painted on and low-pitched roofs and chimneys were added. Interior staircases were put in to make all the rooms accessible to each other. The houses were made smaller and lighter and although they still opened like a cupboard they no longer carried locks. Occasionally they were given iron handles for easy lifting. As all these new developments were incorporated baby-houses were seen more often in the nursery and less frequently in the drawing room.

In 1801 Maria Edgeworth could write in *Practical Education* that 'an unfinished baby-house might be a good toy, as it would employ little carpenters and sempstresses to fit it up, but a completely finished baby-house proves as tiresome to a child as a finished seat to a young nobleman.' The concept of imaginative, creative play with an accessible dolls' house seems not to have occurred to her. However, the 19th century, as we

have seen, brought great changes in the way that children were treated, and this influenced the development of dolls' houses. As the century advanced, bringing with it the golden, sentimental age of childhood, more sophisticated manufacturing and production techniques were applied to these houses. Fewer were made by estate carpenters; their contents and furniture ceased to be the prized work of individual craftsmen and were soon being mass-produced all over Europe.

By the end of the 19th century dolls' houses were widely available. The British product, usually factory-made, tended to be cheap and crude, while much finer examples were imported from northern Europe. All houses tended to resemble real houses, with the neoclassical country house giving way to the fashionable Gothic influence with towers and balconies. Their interiors were usually an accurate representation of the crowded, claustrophobic homes of Victorian England. Many different types of house were imitated at this time from the tiny cottage to the formal town house.

French dolls' houses of the 19th century reflect French styles of architecture, with their extravagant delight in exterior decoration. Those of the 1870s and 1880s often have gabling and mansard or French windows. It is interesting to note that most English, German and French houses contained a well-equipped kitchen. Bathrooms began to appear and some of the most sumptuous houses had lifts and coach-houses attached to them and sometimes small gardens. Even small houses possessed up to six rooms and, by now, a staircase was a regular feature in all of them.

Although every child, no matter how poor, could have a doll of some kind, dolls' houses remained beyond the reach of the poor, and were seen as a symbol of privilege. The size of a dolls' house means that there must be room to keep it in the home; its furnishings and decoration imply that the owner has the time and money to lavish on a hobby. A little girl today can play with her own dolls' house, which will probably be small, compact and portable, not much taller than she is. It may be furnished

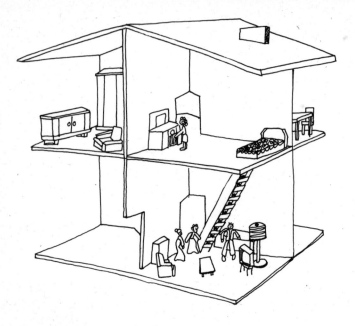

Modern toy; the absence of exterior walls makes the contents of the house more accessible

with ill-assorted bits and pieces with a rudimentary lighting system wired up to all too evident batteries. These defects are irrelevant to the child's pleasure; for her the house represents a whole world to organize as she will.

How would a little girl from a high-rise flat, a suburban street or a bungalow regard the huge Palladian-fronted house at Uppark in England? It is certainly recognizable as a dolls' house but it stands high on a base, made in imitation of the piazza Inigo Jones designed for Covent Garden in London. It opens like a cupboard to reveal nine rooms, each elegantly furnished in great detail. There is no bathroom, but the kitchen is well equipped with its *batterie de cuisine*; there are canopied beds, oil paintings and brass locks on the doors. The entire piece is surmounted by a balustraded pediment on which seven statues stand poised. A little girl would probably be too small to see more than the rooms on the first floor. Should she feel an urge to rearrange the furniture, or to remove and examine all the tiny treasures, even if she were not intimidated by the overall size and splendour of the house, it would be hard to approach it in any relaxed way.

The fashion for individual room-settings made a brief reappearance in the 19th century, although they were now designed to amuse children rather than to be displayed by ladies of fashion. There were dolls' schoolrooms, playgrounds, and even dolls' churches. And, of course, the dolls' shop which provided a wonderful opportunity for inventive play and could be said to train children in the use of money and instil some basic arithmetic. For the collector their attraction lies in their abundance of miniature replicas of almost every saleable item from food to books. There are records of dolls' shops in existence as early as the 17th century in France and Germany but it seems that they were never intended to be used as playthings. Until the 19th century shopping as we now know it was not possible; the pedlar dolls of the 18th century were replaced by the toy shop. The French made toy shops full of miniature fashionable clothes, while the British made some very attractive butchers' shops with their glowing sides of beef and jolly salesmen.

Houses of special interest

Many famous houses have remained within the same family for generations, being elaborated and extended with each succeeding generation. This often leads to rooms of Georgian design or Victorian décor, for example, being furnished in a modern style; in the same way in the family home the modern is blended with the established to create a comfortable pattern of living. We owe the survival of so many beautiful houses to the loving care that adults lavished on them. 18th century baby-houses have usually survived since they were primarily regarded as furniture, although even they were sometimes disregarded and thrown out. Today's collectors are delighted to discover derelict dolls' houses which they can repair and refurbish. Searching out just the right furniture and accessories and assembling them provides an absorbing hobby for both men and women.

If a dolls' house survives the period of neglect between child's plaything and adult's hobby its future is secure. A particularly fine example of a house that survived this transitional period is the Graham Montgomery house in the Museum of Childhood in Edinburgh. It began life in 1897 when Mrs Graham Montgomery was four, and she was its sole owner until her death in 1955. The house is seven feet long and five feet high. Its exterior is modelled on the house in Hampshire where she lived and looks, at the back, like an Elizabethan-style manor, with door, windows and tower. The front, however, makes no concessions to the imitation of reality and is simply a series of glass-fronted cabinets; three of these cabinets are linked and, having a staircase, look like a section through a real house. The fourth cabinet is not attached to the others, has no staircase, and therefore appears as a simple display case. The house contains some 18 rooms: guest-room, modern girls' room (created in 1930), schoolroom, playroom, vintage bathroom, glory hole (for lumber), master-bedroom and one other bedroom, drawing-room, dining-room, library, Chinese room, night nursery and maid's room, as well as, of course, a main

Early idealized baby doll

hall and a wide staircase with two landings. There are more than 2,000 individual items in this house including some extremely valuable and rare objects. There are books in the library, things to eat in the kitchen, medicines in the bathroom and even a stack of appropriate things in the glory hole. The house contains a grand piano and other tiny instruments. There is electric light throughout and a water system, both of which have caused near-disasters at times. The Graham Montgomery house is perhaps an ideal dolls' house and has enjoyed an ideal life.

The 20th century has not been distinguished for its production of dolls' houses, and many experts reject the modern product out of hand although there are some well-made examples on sale today. There have been some interesting individual houses made, however, with garages, lifts, swimming pools, roof gardens and many 20th century innovations. One house, in London's Bethnal Green Museum, is prepared for war with an Anderson bomb-shelter in the garden and tape on the glass windows to prevent a spray of fragments should the glass be shattered by an explosion.

Throughout the years custom-built houses have been commissioned on a spectacular scale. One of the most famous is that which Sir Edward Lutyens designed for Queen Mary in the 1920s. This is displayed at Windsor Castle and is full of miniatures in perfect scale, executed by England's finest craftsmen. In similar style is the

house known as Titania's Palace made by Sir Nevile Wilkinson for his daughter. It was begun in 1907 and finished 15 years later. Neither of these superb palaces was intended to be a toy and should be judged as a work of art rather than a toy.

Constant reference has been made in this introduction to the charm of the miniature accessories with which dolls' houses have been furnished and decorated. This can almost be classed as a separate field of interest for there are many who collect miniature objects without having a house to put them in. Certainly every single item that could possibly be found in house or shop has, at one time or another, been reproduced in miniature. After the middle of the 19th century the quality of small pieces is less fine but until then most dolls' houses contained valuable and luxurious items. Baby-houses were even made expressly to display collections of silver, gold or ivory miniatures. Special collections of dolls' house furniture which included all kinds of objects from piano to whatnot were devised; these are often very highly prized by collectors today.

The golden age of dolls' houses seems to have passed, just as the golden age of gracious living has disappeared. Surviving dolls' houses from past eras are now classed as antiques. All the dolls' houses we can examine in the great museums of the world and in private collections are a constant reminder of a life-style we can never recapture.

Selected reading list

Coleman, Dorothy S., Elizabeth A. and Evelyn J. *The Collector's Encyclopedia of Dolls* Robert Hale, London, 1970; Crown, New York, 1968.

Desmonde, Kay *Dolls and Dolls' Houses* Letts, London, 1972.

Flick, Pauline *Toys and Toy Museums* Shire Publications, Aylesbury, 1971.

Fraser, Antonia *Dolls* Weidenfeld & Nicolson, London, 1963; Putnam, New York, 1963.

Greene, Vivien *English Dolls' Houses of the Eighteenth and Nineteenth Centuries* Batsford, London, 1955.

Latham, Jean *Dolls' Houses* Black, London, 1969; Scribner, New York, 1969.

Murray, Patrick *Toys* Studio Vista, London, 1968; Dutton, New York, 1968.

Index to photographs

1 *Ushabti* grave figures dating from 1900 BC. These small figures, which are among the earliest known, were discovered in Egyptian tombs. For a long time it was assumed that they were dolls but they are now thought to be representations of the servants of the deceased, placed in his grave to serve him in the after-life

2 Early grave figure from Roman Egypt, about 2,000 years old

3 Grave doll of about AD 400. This figure was almost certainly a real toy, much loved by the child with whom it was buried

4 This carved wooden doll was made in England at the beginning of the 17th century. The plain dress with its deep collar illustrates the severity of Puritan costume

5 Detail of 'La Carita' by Lucas Cranach (1472-1553). This is one of the earliest paintings in which we can see a doll used by a child as a plaything. The doll that the little girl holds here is another stiff, formally dressed figure and makes a sharp contrast to the generally relaxed atmosphere of the painting

7

6 Dutch dolls' house of the late 17th century. In all countries of Northern Europe the dolls' house followed the same pattern of development, being first a display cabinet, then a baby-house and finally a dolls' house for children to play with. This is a particularly fine example of an early cabinet. It is just a collection of rooms without a staircase to link them; no attempt has been made to imitate the exterior of a real house. Each room has its own distinctive character, from the laundry on the top floor to the kitchen on the ground floor. Small dolls can be seen performing their allotted household tasks

7 Nuremberg dolls' house of 1673 – a very early and rudimentary form of dolls' house. It is fully equipped and opens like a cupboard but is only 3 feet 6 inches high. It contains stoves and has chimneys but there is no staircase. Most of the contents of this house are contemporary and include a high, curtained bed, a stocking-stretcher and even a baby-walker. Perhaps the most interesting feature of the house is the equipment for the rooms downstairs which includes all the contents of the famous Nuremberg kitchens: *batterie de cuisine*, hen-coop, scales and innumerable pots, pans, plates, cups and basins

8 English wooden doll of about 1700. She has a carved and painted head and patches on her face – a fashionable affectation of the time. She is said to have been given by the family of the Old Pretender to the English throne, James Stuart, to one of their loyalist supporters

9 Wooden doll dressed in the style of 1710; she has fashionably arched eyebrows and highly coloured cheeks

10 English wooden dolls of the mid-17th century. The one on the right is marked on the body 'dressed in the fashion 1763'

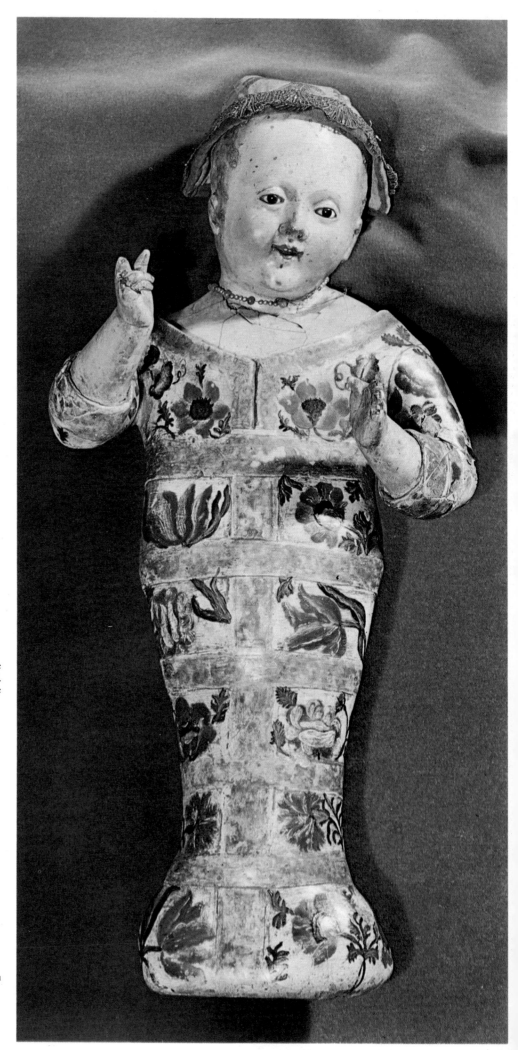

11   This beautifully preserved Italian doll of the mid-18th century is over 24 inches high. She is made from composition over wood and delicately painted. A necklace and a bonnet made of material complete her fine appearance

12   Mechanical musical dolls made in Italy in the 18th century. The Italians were particularly adept at devising elegant groups of dolls activated by mechanical devices. They often made dolls representing famous religious or political figures, and a large doll factory was established in Milan in 1909. Italian craftsmen took their skills all over the world; for example, Pierotti, who worked in England, came from a family that made religious figures in wax in Italy

13   Early English dolls' house (1730-40) in a mahogany cabinet with a lock. Already the outside of the cabinet has been made to look like a house, with a door and windows, but there are as yet no roof or chimneys. This piece of furniture is of the sort used to house collections of miniature silverware or porcelain as well as furniture

14   Cane End house was designed about 1756 in the workshops of the great 18th century English furniture-maker, Chippendale, for the Vanderstegen family of Reading, England. The staircase is a particularly fine example of miniature craftsmanship. Chippendale also made the original furniture but unfortunately it is no longer with the dolls' house

15 Nativity tableau from France, executed in Nevers glass. The French tradition of model crèches reached a peak of popularity at the end of the 18th century

16 Tate baby-house – a particularly fine example of a mid-18th century English dolls' house. It is large (7 feet 2 inches high) and made of mahogany; both of its wing doors can be locked. Made for a family called Tate in about 1760, it represents a departure from display cabinets and quite possibly imitates the architectural style of the family house itself. Particularly interesting are the fine outdoor flights of steps, the lantern on the roof, which lights the staircase and hall, the Venetian window, the balustrade and the circular windows. The interior of the house is delightfully equipped

17 This fine 18th century wooden doll recently changed hands for a world record price of £1,000. It is a particularly good example of English dolls of the time of George III and has a turned body with a painted head. The eyes, which are set in the head, are brown enamel, the wooden hands are forked and the legs are pointed; the doll is 19 inches high. She is wearing contemporary clothes and printed cotton underclothing. She has two necklaces – one coral, the other of seed pearls and black glass beads – and is wearing a straw sun bonnet. Such dolls were extremely popular in England and Germany

16

17

18 Three of the most popular types of doll available in early Victorian England. On the left a doll of 1827 with a papier mâché head wears contemporary costume. Papier mâché was widely used since it was cheap to produce and almost indestructible. Notice how the hair of this doll is moulded with the face and neck in the extravagant style of the age; these dolls were often called milliner's dolls for this reason. The one in the centre has a china head with a delicately tinted glaze. Dolls were often made to resemble the famous, and this doll was modelled on Princess Alexandra, who later became Queen of England. The doll on the right is made of wax and dated 1830 but here she is dressed in the fashion of a later period

19 A pair of early 19th century pedlar dolls. Pedlar dolls, made in Britain from the early 18th century, have a unique fascination and are now highly prized by collectors. Usually they are made of wood but this pair have kid heads with woollen hair. Pedlars were familiar figures in the English countryside from the Middle Ages, and country children used to make their own versions using apples for heads. The pedlar doll is interesting because it shows us what the working class of the period looked like, in sharp contrast to the contemporary fashion dolls. The doll's tray shows us the type of merchandise sold by pedlars – almost everything from sheets of music to braces. This pair is specially interesting as the man is a market gardener and the woman a poultry seller. He balances a basket of flowers on his straw hat and carries an oval basket of garden produce that includes carrots, onions and seeds; she carries one basket of hens and another of eggs and dairy produce. He is 10 inches

high; she is 8½ inches high. Each stands on a circular base and has a glass dome for protection – an indication that they were prized as ornaments

20 This pair of pedlar dolls, also dating from the early 19th century, have leather heads with glass bead eyes. They are offering a variety of haberdashery and trinkets

21 Group of dolls dressed by the young Queen Victoria to represent famous figures of the day. They are small, jointed wooden dolls, usually known as Dutch dolls although they were in fact German

22 German wax dolls with cloth bodies dating from about 1830. Such dolls, with their crudely painted faces, could be bought at market stalls

20

22

 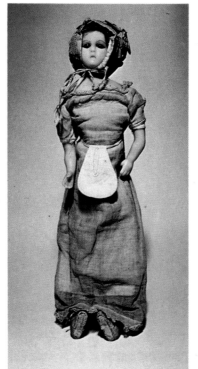 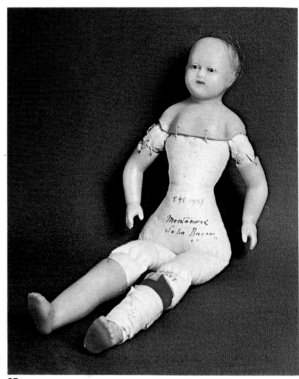

23   24   25

26

23 Small English wax doll of about 1840 with hair painted on the head

24 Early 19th century doll with a wax head and arms attached to a cloth body. The outer dress has been lost but her apron remains

25 Wax doll of about 1850 in the best English tradition of wax modelling as established by the Italian firms of Montanari and Pierotti. This doll was modelled on Queen Victoria's daughter, Princess Louise. The body is stuffed cloth and you can see the stitches that join it to the limbs and head. This kind of doll gave rise to the expression 'I'm up to dolly's wax' meaning that the speaker could eat no more

26 Three glazed porcelain heads for dolls dating from the mid-19th century. China heads which were developed in Germany became very popular at this time. The hair was usually coloured black as in these examples, but some heads were produced without any hair and a place on the crown to which a wig could be fitted. Unglazed china is called bisque (a contraction of the 'biscuit mix' used to make china). When heads were made with no colouring matter at all the material was known as Parian since it resembled the white marble of the island of Paros. Bisque and Parian are essentially the same material

27 Frozen Charlottes – the name given to very small dolls executed in glass or unglazed porcelain and moulded in one piece. They can measure anything from $\frac{3}{4}$ inch to 12 inches, and their arms may be bent at the elbow or moulded to the body. Produced from about 1850 to the beginning of the present century, they are frequently to be found in trays of miscellaneous goods in antique shops or on market stalls. The male version of these dolls was known as a Frozen Charlie

28 Town house of the period 1840-50. Here the need to put a dolls' house on a stand led to the space below being filled in to form a basement. At this time many houses of this type were being built in London

29

29 An unusual example of a piece of furniture used as a display case for models of beautifully furnished rooms. The soft furnishings and the dolls' clothes were made by the wife and daughters of the owner of the house, a Manchester doctor, between 1835 and 1838. The house clearly provided an interesting hobby for them. The drawing-room contains a collection of miniature toys, and there is food in the kitchen, and even a pork pie baking in the oven

30 Rubber doll of 1840 – a very early example of experimentation with unbreakable materials. Rubber was not used extensively for dolls until this century

30

32

31-3 Dolls dressed in national costume are not new to the 20th century. The exotic costumes of foreign lands were as attractive in the mid-19th century as they are today. Here are a pair of Canadian, probably Eskimo dolls, a Welsh woman and a splendid Russian gentleman – all made in Germany

33

34   Paper dressing doll set from Germany of about 1850. These beautifully designed, colourful books of cut-out figures with a range of different dresses for the basic doll originated in Germany and were soon popular all over Europe

35   English wax baby doll, about 1850, made by Madame Montanari. Until this time doll manufacturers had not attempted to delineate the age of a doll; Madame Montanari, a leading London doll-maker of Italian extraction, was the first to make dolls looking like babies. They soon captured the public imagination and were manufactured in large numbers

36   German wax doll of the 1840s (wearing a dress made for her some 30 years later). The head and shoulders are moulded wax, the body is stuffed cloth and the limbs are covered in kid – a typical combination of materials of the time

37   French fashion doll of the 1870s with a bisque head

38   German wax doll of about 1850, with kid-covered limbs

39

40

41 42

39 Pair of wax dolls from a German factory, about 1870. Boy dolls, of which this is a very well-preserved example, were always comparatively rare

40-42 Three elegant dolls of French origin dating from the 1870s; two have bisque heads, while the doll dressed in purple is made of wax

43 Bisque doll from Germany, about 1865. The delicate colouring of her face was very fashionable in the mid-19th century. Her dress probably dates from the end of the century

44 English bisque-headed doll of the 1870s

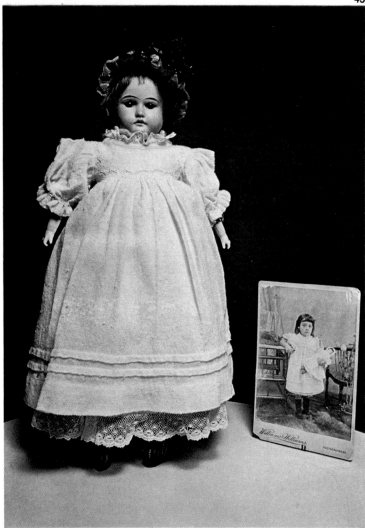

45-6 Two German dolls of the 1880s pictured with their owners. Both dolls are dressed in imitation of their owners' costumes – a popular conceit of the period

47 Graham Montgomery house – one of the most spectacular of all dolls' houses. It is 7 feet long and 5 feet high, has some 18 rooms, a hall and a staircase. It was modelled on a house in Hampshire, England, and is in the architectural style of an Elizabethan mansion. It was the property of Mrs Graham Montgomery, who began to furnish it in 1897 when she was four years old. She retained her interest in the house throughout her life, and it contains one of the largest collections of dolls' house furniture, ornaments, *objets d'art* and soft furnishings. The attic is even filled with discarded objects. The house has both electric light and a water supply

48 Music room in the Graham Montgomery house. It contains a French grand piano and pianola, a mandolin and a guitar, as well as a fine set of chairs with Tonbridge-ware backs

49 1930s room created in the Graham Montgomery house for a growing daughter. Here the atmosphere is more casual; there is a miniature edition of a social magazine, the *Tatler*, on the floor

50 Detail of an interesting 19th century dolls' house, showing a glass conservatory behind a glass bead curtain leading from the main drawing room of the house. Notice the flourishing hot-house plants

51 A German bisque doll of the 1890s, dressed to go out walking

52 German dolls' house furniture of the late 19th century. The fireplace, chairs and mirrored side table are all made from metal

53 Set of miniature furniture of the kind produced in France during the last half of the 19th century. Each piece is decorated with an intricate floral transfer pattern. There are birds above the clock and cherubs support the looking-glass. Miniature objects such as these are collector's items in their own right

54 English wax doll of the 1880s, dressed for a special function at court. She is carrying a fan and a tiny pair of gloves

55 Dolls dressed as brides have always been popular. This is a German example dating from the 1890s and made of wax

52

53

54

56-7 Here are some examples of the wide range of clothes and accessories that were created for dolls in the 19th century. A doll's wardrobe might include every item of adult dress, even a corset, and she was expected to carry gloves for formal occasions and a parasol if necessary

58 Simple Dutch dolls remained popular throughout the 19th century; they were comparatively cheap and durable. This doll dates from the late 1880s and is dressed in Flemish costume

59 Group of 19th century wooden dolls, which shows how they varied in size and how they were jointed. The doll on the left appears rather badly injured; it was used to illustrate a murder in an American piracy trial

60

61

62

60 Simply carved but charming and full of character, this American wooden doll of about 1880 has movable arms

61 Such age-old traditional figures as Mr Punch often turned up in the nursery. This papier mâché doll of about 1875 has the humped back and peascod stomach of Punch and contains a squeaking device

62 Fine example of a Jumeau doll. The Jumeau factory in France was the largest doll-making establishment in the world in the 19th century; it specialized in the production of bisque dolls of exceptionally high quality which won prizes at exhibitions in Paris, London, Vienna, New Orleans and Antwerp

63 Two costume dolls representing the southern United States made from stuffed black cotton with embroidered eyes and lips. They are one foot high and were made in Ireland in the late 19th century. Ethnic dolls – of a very different kind – are again being produced today

64 The 19th century saw many experiments in doll-making. Several firms came up with a walking doll; the most famous of these, patented in America in the middle of the century, was called the Autoperipatetikos. These dolls could be made to walk on their own either by being wound up or by the action of a lever to move the feet – as in this fine example

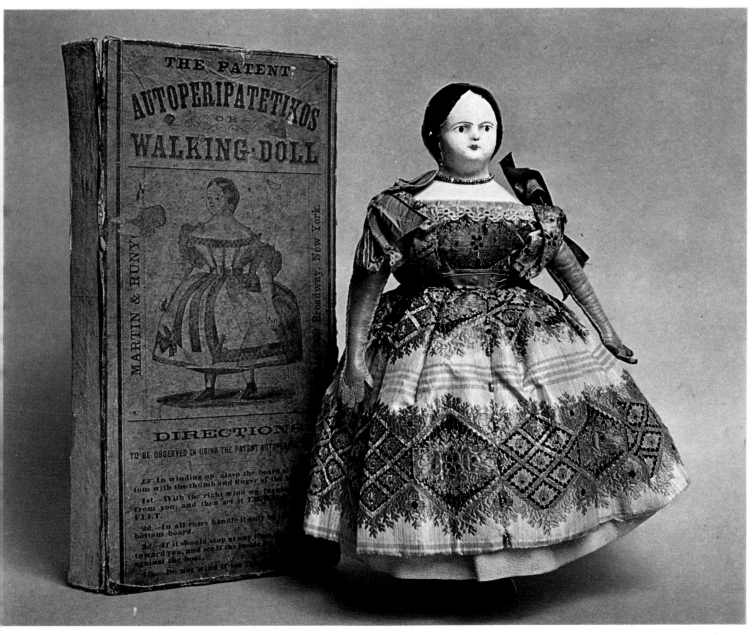

65

66

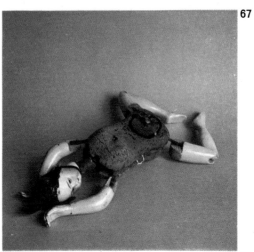

67

65 This elaborate walking doll, dated 1870, is French; a clockwork mechanism moves her arms, wheels her forward and squeezes a bellows which makes her say 'mama'

66 Dolls representing negroes were often used in the construction of automata, sometimes as servants in attendance (as in the famous Italian musical groups of the 18th century) and later as entertainers, like this pair of dancers. These dancers have jointed bodies and painted heads; there is a mechanism in their box which operates the posts on which they hang to make them perform a tap dance routine

67 Amusing inventions abounded in the 19th century, such as this swimming doll. It has a cork body and jointed limbs and when wound up performs a jerky backstroke

68 Flirting-eyed doll made about 1910 by the German factory of Simon and Halberg which specialized in distinctive dolls' faces. She has a papier mâché body, and a bisque head with blue eyes, parted lips and pierced ears. She is 22 inches high and can walk and squeak as well as flutter her eyelashes

68

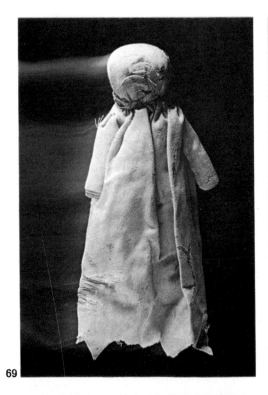

69

70

69 Dolls have often been given a ritual significance. This is a ghost doll from France; it represented the deceased person and was carried by mourners or placed in the house of the deceased, usually for a year, to guard his spirit as it made the journey from this world to the next; it was then burned on the anniversary of the death

70 Spirit doll from West Africa, date unknown. Here dolls have maintained a strong association with the occult, right up to the present day

71 Balinese doll made from dried palm leaves probably dating from the end of the 19th century. Such figures originally made for religious purposes were later given to children to play with. (The small palm trees are probably British, made from alloy and date from the 1920s)

73

74

72 Voodoo doll from the West Indies. Dolls have been used in witchcraft for many centuries, and this contemporary one was designed for inflicting harm on people

73 Not all children are lucky enough to possess beautiful, manufactured dolls; and there is a long tradition going back to Roman times of making dolls out of any available material. Rag dolls belong to this tradition, as do dolls made from household objects such as spoons and pestles. These dolls, which have grown from the emotional needs of children, are known as 'emergent' dolls. This particular example of an emergent doll was created by an Edinburgh child in 1965 from scraps of material and newspaper

74 Emergent doll made from an old shoe and ingeniously dressed. It was found in a London slum district in the 1890s

75 Shop-sign doll, also made from any available materials, from Normandy, late 19th century. It was appropriately used to advertise the shop of a rag-and-bone merchant

76 From left to right this group of ethnic dolls includes two Chinese and Mandalay balance figures, a Guatemalan water carrier, a Peruvian female figure, a Chinese horseman and a Mexican religious toy

77 Sword-play dolls from Japan, dating from the 1880s. Unfortunately their weapons are missing

77

78-9 Japanese *kokeshi* dolls, traditionally offerings to the gods made by childless women in the hope of being blessed with fertility. The miniature *kokeshi* dolls are made from single grains of rice; their heads are movable but cannot be separated from the body. These modern examples are made for children to play with

80-81 Two American Indian dolls; the one with the realistic face is modern and made for tourists, the other, which dates from the 1880s, is dressed as a member of the Sioux

82

82 Three 20th century Eskimo dolls made of cloth. They form part of the tradition of rag dolls, which is as old as history and still very much alive today

83 Modern Russian nest of dolls. These gaily painted little figures fit into each other and are of traditional design

84 Russian doll made of moss of the late 19th century

83

84

85

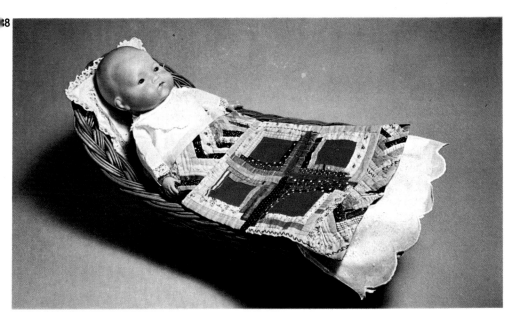

85   Charming German bisque-headed doll of about 1900, properly dressed to go out visiting

86   German doll made between 1900 and 1905; the head is bisque with fixed brown eyes and pierced ears, the jointed body is of papier mâché (25 inches high)

87   American rag doll of the early 20th century which has obviously enjoyed its owner's affection. Rag dolls were particularly popular at this time. Some American examples dating from the 1870s are now valued highly by collectors

88-9   Two German baby dolls of the first decade of this century. They make an interesting contrast; the first, lying in its cot (the coverlet of which dates from 1850), represents an idealized baby, whereas the second – though less attractive – shows some attempt to portray a real baby. Realistic baby dolls became popular, especially in America, and were often known as character dolls

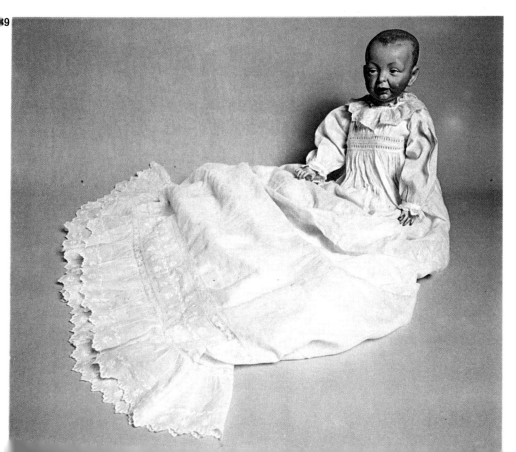

90-91 Two portrait dolls. The female doll, probably made in Germany, is wearing coronation robes of 1911; her identity is unknown. The wax soldier doll, made by Pierotti, is a likeness of Lord Kitchener, dating from 1905. Dolls representing real people were popular throughout the 19th century, and royal families today still attract portrait doll-makers

92 Kewpie dolls, with characteristically cheeky faces and pointed quiff of hair; they were made from various materials including bisque and rubber. In 1913 the name was registered as a trade mark in the United States, Britain and France, following which Kewpie dolls enjoyed a short wave of popularity

93 'The smallest doll in the world' – a popular toy in the early years of the 20th century. At half an inch high, however, it is substantially larger than many other dolls

94 Comparatively modern example of a Nuremberg kitchen. Originating in Nuremberg, these small model kitchens were subsequently made all over the world but retained the generic name. This 1900 example is actually German but by the end of the 19th century it was the Americans who had virtually cornered the market in Nuremberg kitchens

90   91

94

95

96

97

95 English butcher's shop of about 1900. The miniature butcher's shop seems to be a peculiarly British phenomenon; the Americans, who were the first to introduce miniature dummies of branded goods, and actual miniature samples, seem to have preferred general stores and grocery shops. Toy shops are in the same tradition as individual room-settings, providing a similar opportunity to display fascinating collections of miniature objects. This particular example, with its highly coloured cuts of meat hanging up and its jolly butcher carving meat on a block, is typical of the high standard of craftsmanship that went into the making of these models. The coat of arms, which has been added to suggest royal patronage, is in fact a badge of the Household Cavalry regiment

96 English toy shop made after World War I by ex-service men

97 Fully furnished 1930s dolls' house, which has no pretentions to being a collector's item. Clearly those who owned it enjoyed playing with it, and it contains a comfortable mixture of home-made furniture, specially made miniatures and make-do effects. In the kitchen the sink is full of dishes; in the nursery there is a nurse and a baby with its own tiny doll; and in the drawing room two ladies take tea, while their cat snoozes under the table. It is altogether a most delightful toy

59

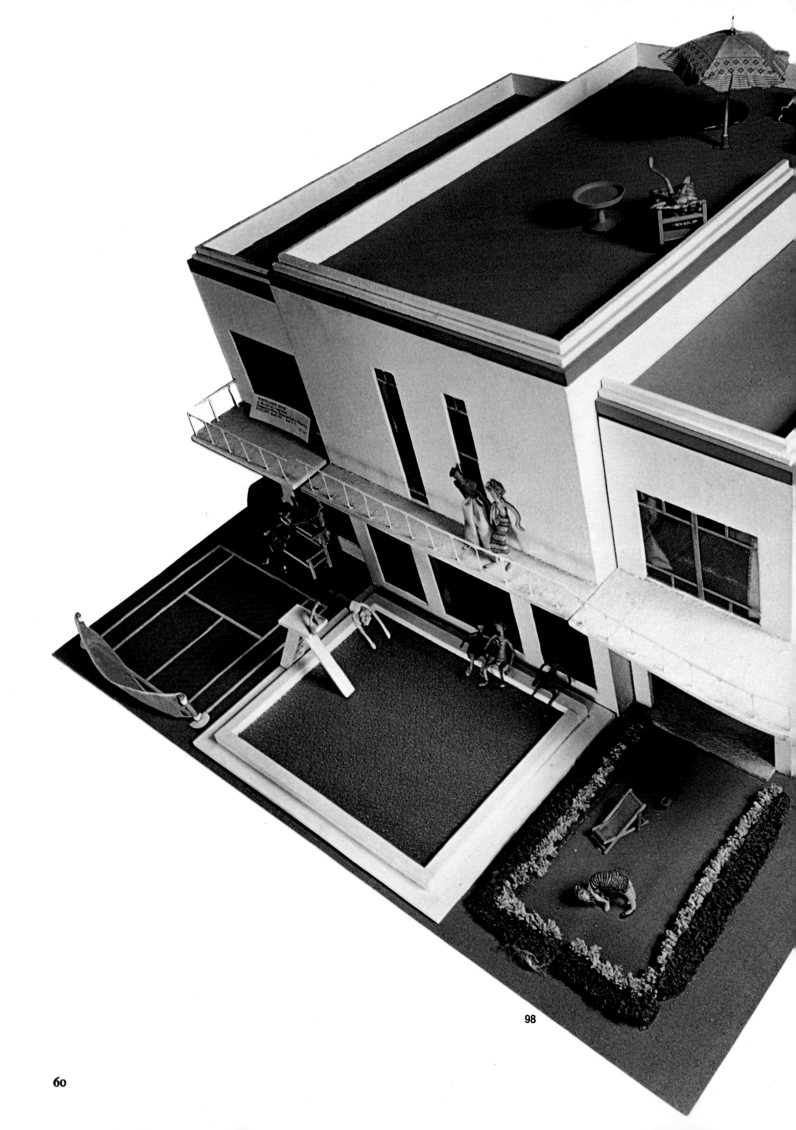

98

98 Whiteladies house, designed in 1935 in imitation of a road-house. It certainly has captured the atmosphere of the thirties, with its flat roof equipped for sunbathing, the pool into which a small doll is forever diving, the tennis court and the indolent doll lazing in the sun

99 Modern bride doll, made of plastic. She differs very little from her 19th century forerunner (see page 41)

100 Some modern dolls made to represent flowers; the ingenuity of doll-makers is clearly not yet exhausted

101 Action Man – one of the most successful of contemporary toys, with a strong appeal to boys. Action Man can be made to take part in a wide variety of activities – sets of clothes and equipment, sold separately, will turn the basic doll into soldier, sailor (seen here), mountaineer, show jumper or other heroic figure

102 Fashion doll – 1970s style. This is Daisy, a doll you can dress, devised by international fashion designer Mary Quant for mass-production. Daisy has the long legs and luxuriant blonde hair of the fashion model; she is made of rubber and is 9 inches high. With a choice of 36 different outfits she is equipped for almost every occasion

103 Two modern Scottish costume dolls

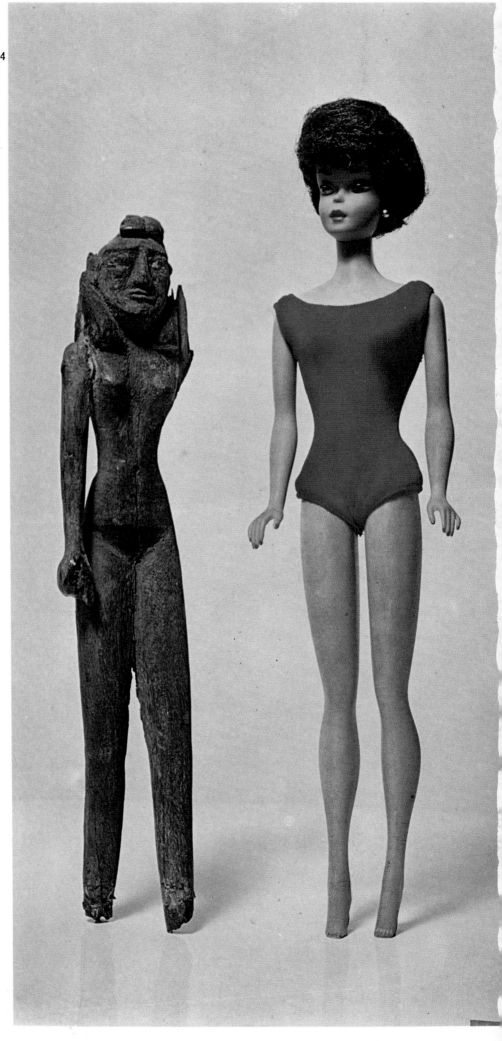

104 Almost 4,000 years separate these two dolls –
an Egyptian grave doll of about 2000 BC and a
plastic doll very much of the 1960s